Boulevard

Boule

NATHANAEL O'REILLY

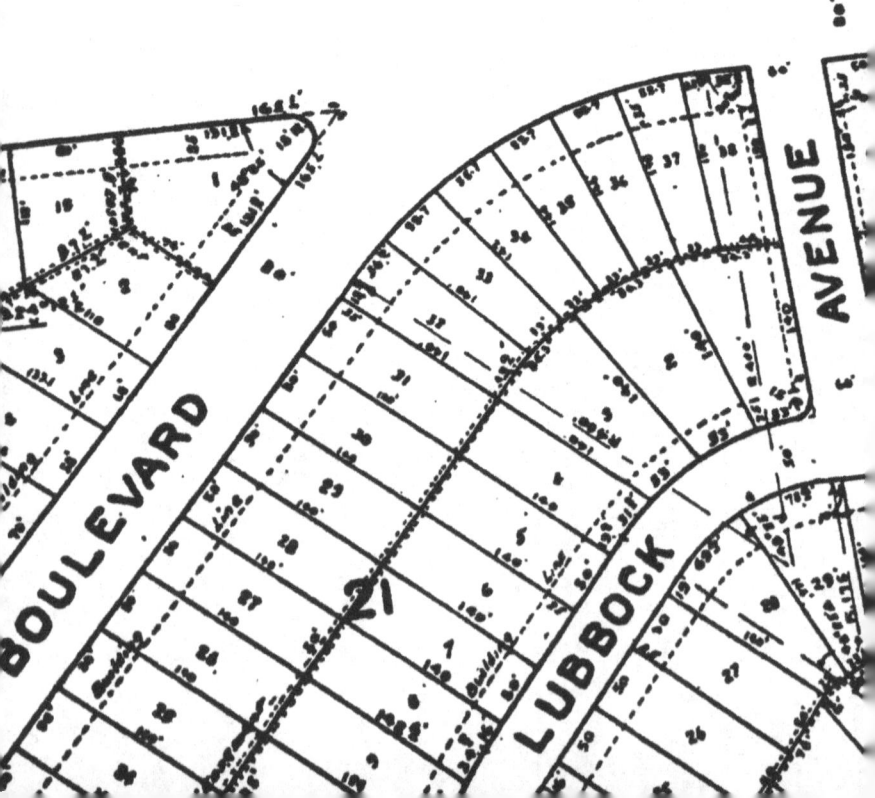

vard

Downingfield Press

Words copyright © 2023 Nathanael O'Reilly.
Typesetting and book design copyright © 2023
Downingfield Press Proprietary Limited.
All rights reserved.

Without limiting the rights under copyright reserved above, in accordance with the
Copyright Act 1968 (Commonwealth of Australia) no part of this publication may be
reproduced, stored in or introduced into a retrieval system, or transmitted, in any form
or by any means (electronic, mechanical, xerographic, recording, or otherwise), without
the prior written permission of the copyright owner and the publisher of this book.

Nathanael O'Reilly asserts their right to be
known as the author of this work.

First published September 2021
Acquired and published February 2024 by
DOWNINGFIELD PRESS PROPRIETARY LIMITED
Suite 346
585 Little Collins Street
Melbourne Victoria 3000

mail@downingfield.com · www.downingfield.com

Downingfield Press undertakes its work on the unceded lands of the Wurundjeri people
of the Kulin Nation and pays respect to Elders past, present, and emerging.

ISBN 978-0-6452318-5-4 (paperback)
ISBN 978-0-6452318-6-1 (epub)

Cover and book design by M. G. Mader

A catalogue record for this
work is available from the
National Library of Australia

INTRODUCTION

Boulevard is a product of the Covid-19 pandemic. Unable to travel to Australia and Ireland (my homelands), and forced to work from home for almost a year, I turned my attention to the hyperlocal. *Boulevard* is a book-length poem in 76 sections. Or maybe it's a collection of 76 numbered poems that can each be read as stand-alone works. That's not for me to decide. The work belongs to the reader now. *Boulevard* explores the life of a street and neighbourhood over the course of a year during the pandemic. I forced myself to write about events happening in front of my house, in nearby backyards, a couple of blocks to the east and west along the boulevard. Instead of travelling in search of subject matter, poetry came to me. Surprising, beautiful and sometimes shocking events took place outside my window. I focused on my immediate surroundings, rather than my distant homelands, my past, my loved ones overseas. I took inspiration from Basil Bunting's *Briggflatts* and Alex Lemon's *Another Last Day* (written and set just a few blocks to my west), both book-length poems devoted to the local. I found the poetry in the everyday, the seemingly normal and ordinary. I came to know the birds, squirrels, cats, dogs and trees. I learnt the rhythms of the days, detailed the changing of the seasons, experienced the unexpected. And yet I always did so as an immigrant, a foreigner, an exile, bestriding the boundary between insider and outsider.

1

live oaks cast shadows across

manicured lawns, carefully-

edged curbs, asphalt-filled potholes

brown metal water meter

covers, cracked concrete driveways

parked late-model SUVs

leaf-strewn gutters, wooden

powerline poles, overgrown

alleys, cedar paling fences

stone retaining walls, wrought iron

gates & railings, black metal

mailboxes, NO PARKING, SPEED

HUMPS AHEAD & STOP signs

recycling bins, air conditioning

units, interrupted sidewalks

trimmed hedges, flowerbeds

garages & garage apartments

backyard swimming pools, hot tubs

garden sheds, BBQs, patio

furniture, firepits, crushed quartz

red Adirondack chairs, paved

pathways, fenced-in dogs, hammocks

vegetable gardens, palm trees

a rack of deer antlers attached

to a backyard garage, magnolias

beeches & crepe myrtles, al fresco

dining zones, potted herbs, sunbeds

American flags, beer-pong tables

Buffalo & Bermuda grass, squirrels

cats, horned frogs and geckos

2

a tall, slim, grey-haired man

in his sixties, wearing

a red cap, blue jeans, brown

boat shoes & a white long-

sleeved t-shirt examines

the boulevard's gutters

at dawn, picks up plastic

cups, empty cans, water

bottles, scraps of junk mail

deposits trash in bins

parked behind garages

in alleys, arranges

garbage & recycling

bins into neater rows

shapes the environment

within view of his home

exerts control over

his visual domain, lifts

the neighborhood single-

handedly to his standard

3

workers with a jackhammer

destroy the concrete path

connecting the sidewalk

to a front door, load chunks

of concrete into a trailer.

the crepe myrtle blooms

with fragrant white flowers

beneath cloudless blue skies

4

the postman walks across front lawns

from letterbox to letterbox

EarPods inserted, chatting

to friends, laughing & smiling

waves to homeowners sitting

at desks facing front windows

working remotely during

the pandemic, delivers

news, bills & junk mail

brings the world to the isolated

5

the house on the eastern corner

of Greene & the boulevard

sits empty, fallen branches

drying & cracking on the roof

like sheep skeletons in the sun

weeds colonizing the front yard

grass growing thigh-high, bamboo

blocking the sidewalk, conquering

the backyard, camouflaging

the degenerating garage

6

at the corner of University

& the boulevard a group of twenty-

ish students throw a birthday bash

during lockdown in the parking lot

behind their apartment building

play beer pong & twerk to a pumping

sound system, yeehaa down a twenty-foot-

high inflatable slide, carouse in swim-

suits while the virus kills

7

a neighbor's diesel truck engine
rumbles before dawn as he prepares
to drive west to the oil fields

trees shade ninety-year-old brick houses
single-family homes on the south side
student share-houses on the north side

the doof doof of hip hop bass drums
insists from behind an eight-foot-high
cedar fence, punctuated
by whoops, hollers & hell yeahs

truck brakes squeal & screech as drivers
finally notice the speed hump

8

a blue USPS mailbox

sits on a small triangular

traffic island sharing space

with two crepe myrtles, cactus

a concrete bench & a patch

of unmown wild Bermuda

9

a white Jeep Wrangler

reverses from a driveway

interrupts oncoming traffic

pick-up trucks, SUVs

& sedans get the green light

cross the intersection

at University, accelerate

down the boulevard

towards the stop sign at Waits

rev engines in low gear

oblivious to the camouflaged

speed hump just before Greene

10

green leaves on the live oaks
flutter in the morning breeze

as boughs bounce slowly
in the easterly. a garage

door service van parks outside
Jamie's house, lettering

on the van's side proudly
proclaiming VETERAN

alongside American flags
the morning after the Charter

Cable van parked in the shade
of the same tree's boughs

11

garbage, recycling & yard waste
bins stand in the gutters lining

both sides of the boulevard
on Tuesday evenings & Wednesday

mornings. the first truck arrives
before dawn, wakes sleeping residents

sends a mechanical right arm
out to grasp each bin, lift it ten

feet above the asphalt, inverts
& dumps its contents before
dropping each hollow empty

12

the sound of a beautiful voice
singing floats along the boulevard

as a Beyoncé lookalike
wearing a yellow Kanken backpack

skips past singing like a Broadway
star, dances along the sidewalk

grooving to the soundtrack in her ears
skips, twirls, shuffles, strides, serenades

13

university students

in workout clothing stride along

the boulevard engaged

in urgent conversation

a young man in black jeans

& grey t-shirt stands

on the front steps of a house

talking on a smartphone

cradled against his left ear

ladders, lawnmowers, edgers

leaf blowers & hedge trimmers

rattle & thump in trailers towed

by trucks hitting speed humps

14

the Amazon delivery

woman jumps from the open

door of her idling truck

blasting hip hop beats

runs up the concrete path

to the front door, places

a package on the threshold

snaps a smartphone photo

pounds on the door, turns

skips back to her truck

15

Jamie mows his own lawn

for the first time this year

pushes the mower back

& forth in straight lines

wearing khaki cargo shorts

running shoes, white socks

black t-shirt, grey gardening

gloves, wraparound sunglasses

& black baseball cap, applies

his engineer's mind to a menial task

16

the poet who lives in the house

on the last western block

of the boulevard retreats

inside the house with his wife

& children during the pandemic

emerges alone for pre-dawn exercise

keeps his kids in the backyard

away from the playground

next door where the virus

may linger on swings and slides

17

a student riding

an electric scooter

whizzes towards Kroger

returns fifteen minutes

later with a lone

plastic bag hanging

from the right-hand side

of his handlebars

bulging with secrets

18

a gleaming black Porsche
SUV parked in the driveway

of a two-story student rental
house displays TRUMP 2020

& tri-delt sorority
stickers on its back window

a young man opens the rear
hatch of a parked white Jeep

Cherokee, lifts out two cases
of Michelob Ultra, carries liquid

into the backyard. young couples
dressed in athletic clothes

& sunglasses stroll past along
the sidewalk gripping smartphones

19

a young couple kisses

on their fertile front lawn

while their cute puppy shits.

the man holds a red leash

in one hand, slides his other

onto the woman's ass

20

forty-mile-per-hour winds shake
live oak boughs & branches
vibrate tree crowns, bounce limbs

leaves descend into frontyards
& backyards, onto sidewalks
gusts sway powerlines

as charcoal skies lower
raindrops fall upon parched
lawns, hot paving stones

steaming concrete. cats seek
refuge beneath parked cars
and SUVs. residents

emerge from front doors, perch
on steps, witness the first
rainfall in weeks, reach hands

out to catch condensation

21

young women wearing

cut-off jean shorts, white

tank tops & Aviators

cruise past on skateboards

weave around potholes

acorns & twigs, groove

to tunes transmitted

into wireless headphones

spread life, joy and beauty

22

the morning after a thunder-

storm a live oak limb & branches

heavy enough to kill a person

or crush a car cover a driveway

after snapping off the trunk

falling twenty feet from a neighbor's

tree, averting destruction by inches

& hours, crashing into predawn darkness

23

a black Dodge Charger runs the stop sign

at the corner of Cockrell & the boulevard

slams into the driver's side of a red

PT Cruiser with a cannonball thud

summoning residents running from front

yards. the vehicles sit idle in the street

for a moment of stillness before running

residents reach car doors. a young man

wearing a backwards black baseball cap

& an oversized Cowboys jersey

emerges from the Charger, stands dazed

in the street surveying the damage

while a bearded thirtysomething man

in cargo shorts with a black ponytail

& two golden retrievers on leashes

squats beside the open driver's door

of the Cruiser, gently asks the boomer

driver, *Are you okay, ma'am? Is there*

anything you need? stands up tall, steps

back when she looks at the other driver

yells *What I need is a fuckin' gun!*

24

four white male college

students dressed like middle-

aged golf dads exit

a Tahoe & Jeep

parked in a driveway

pop the trunks, remove

towels & bags of clubs

carry them inside

like fathers carrying

sleeping toddler sons

25

homeowners ease into driveways

in luxury cars, open iron

security gates via remote

control, glide between fences

& houses into double-

garages, close gates behind

themselves, maintain privacy

security and assets

26

a young woman emerges

from a backdoor wrapped in a green

blanket, runs across the boulevard

holding the blanket across her chest

returns twenty seconds later

with a puppy tucked in her armpit

27

in the thirty-three-

hundred block homeowners

install a trampoline

in their backyard

provide an outlet

for their kids' cooped-up

lockdown energy

28

residents keep blinds & curtains

drawn against July afternoon heat

live oak branches reach across

property lines, scrape against

neighboring rooves, drop leaves

& acorns into backyards

a blue jay glides to the iron

handrail, perches briefly, flies

off towards his partner waiting

in the oak above the boulevard

29

a muscular young man

wearing a white t-shirt

grey cargo shorts, a backpack

& a mask strides along

the boulevard, shading

himself with an umbrella

like a geisha with a parasol

30

a blue surgical mask

lies on the grass

beside the gutter

a red-haired teenage boy

mows the front lawn

wearing flip-flops

a thirtysomething white man

with a buzzcut in baggy

jeans & a grey t-shirt

shuffles along the boulevard

clutches a Mellow Mushroom pizza

box with both hands before his belly

31

a fiftysomething man parks
his red dual-cab truck in front
of twenty-nine-twenty-one

gets out, walks to the opposite
side rear passenger door
lets a German Shepherd

on a leash exit the vehicle
squat on the grass & shit
commands the dog to jump

back into the truck, closes
the door, walks back round
to the driver's side, enters

his truck, abandons excrement

32

a tanned, muscular twentysomething

man runs along the boulevard

clutching a t-shirt in his right hand

blonde hair bouncing, sweat

glistening on his arms & torso

a young woman in black booty

shorts & a rainbow tie-dyed

t-shirt parks her grey Civic

in front of her boyfriend's house

skips up the driveway to the backdoor

33

neighborhood cats lounge

in flowerbeds, on doorsteps

beneath parked cars

on lawns in the shade

of oaks & elms

lurk beneath hedges

scamper away from the postman

stalk across green manicured lawns

pursuing insects and lizards

34

a black Dodge SUV

traveling south on Cockrell

blows past the STOP sign

t-bones a silver Dodge coupe

traveling east on the boulevard

seconds after the thump of the impact

residents run into their frontyards

cross into the street & check

on the drivers' condition

a middle-aged white woman

gives a thumbs-up from behind

the deployed airbag in her dented

coupe ceased with the front

end in someone's yard

& the rear end in the gutter

the young male driver of the SUV
exits his vehicle, hustles to the other car
apologizes profusely. bystanders
take out smartphones, dial numbers

residents push the Dodge SUV
out of the intersection, lift a fender
onto the grass. minutes later, a black
& white police SUV arrives

the young uniformed officer
steps out of his vehicle
wearing mirrored sunglasses, dons
a blue surgical facemask, strides
across to the drivers, stands
with hands on hips to hear stories

35

a turbine ventilator on the roof

of a garage apartment rotates

at one-hundred-plus revolutions

per minute, extracts hot, stale

air from the attic, draws fresh

air down into the interior

36

a ginger cat dashes across the street

settles beneath a white Jeep Cherokee

parked in a driveway, lies in the shade

watching passing cars, squirrels

butterflies, birds & insects

a flowering crepe myrtle drops

pink blossoms into a neighboring

swimming pool where they float

in clear water above the bright

blue and white checkered lining

37

a yard sign with a black

background & white font

declares *We Pray for Justice*

empty swings, slides & benches

in the park bake in July heat

For Lease & For Sale signs

appear in front yards commenting

on the pandemic economy

elderly residents water lawns

in the evenings with garden hoses

trim hedges & pull weeds

wave to neighbors from a distance

38

a young woman emerges

from her garage apartment

at dawn in bare feet wearing

a long-sleeved blue denim shirt

bends forward with hands on her

thighs while her labradoodle

puppy lifts his leg, pisses

on the green lawn, stands upright

stretches as he squats, defecates

39

two shirtless young men run along

the boulevard one minute apart

on July fourth, battling ninety-

three-degree heat. minutes later

a third shirtless young man walks past

panting, sweating, hands on hips

seconds later a young red-haired

woman wearing a violet sports

bra & black running shorts glides

past like Diana in pursuit

40

the retired railway worker

installs a massive American

flag on a pole in front of his house

the day before the fourth, grooms

his front yard to patriotic

perfection. the college students

across the street unload plastic chairs

from a pick-up truck, carry stacks

into their backyard, remove trays

of brisket & cases of Bud Light

from their Jeep and Mini Cooper

on the morning of the fourth

41

the driver of a silver

Honda Accord coupe

doesn't see the speed

hump, hits it too quickly

two mountain bikes & rack

fly off the back of the car

crash in a tangled heap

in the middle of the street

42

squirrels pursue each other across

powerlines twenty feet above the verge

an eagle swoops into the oak, attacks

squirrels in flurries of wings & claws

squirrels scamper across the street

narrowly avoid truck tires, take

refuge beneath an Audi A4

43

a blue & white Mini Cooper
parked beneath the live oak gathers
pollen & dust. a red Kia

Soul hatchback reflects the summer
sun, casts a shadow on the cracked
concrete driveway while a white Lexus

SUV prowls the boulevard.
a white Jeep Cherokee & grey
Audi A4 rest in a student

house driveway. a white van with a green
logo & text proclaiming Growth
Solutions cruises the boulevard

turns right. a brand-new white Chevy
Malibu breaks suddenly at the speed
hump, trunk rising, hood dipping

44

wastewater submerges the sidewalk

soaks the lawn & verge

courses into the gutter

as the homeowners drain

their backyard above-ground

pool for the finale

of the pandemic summer

release four thousand gallons

of algae-fouled water

onto the seared boulevard

45

the guardian of the neighborhood
sprays ant-killer into the cracks
between concrete slabs on neighbors'
sidewalks & driveways. a young man

exits a Mini Cooper, opens
the hatch, retrieves a cat carrier
conveys it carefully to his house

a U-Haul parks in a driveway
departs ten minutes later with used
chaise & sofa. the hourly toll

of the campus chapel bell carries
four blocks to the boulevard, divides
residents' days into twenty-four

segments. houses with white-painted brick
walls & red-tiled roofs face each other
across the boulevard. the shadow

of a squirrel scurries across
a stone wall mirroring the movement
of the squirrel across the power-

lines above. BIDEN-HARRIS signs
proliferate in front yards planted
beside driveways, next to curbs, on street

corners. a blue surgical facemask
lies pancaked on the asphalt. vehicles
with out-of-state plates line both sides

of the boulevard. Kentucky,
Minnesota, Iowa, Cali-
fornia, Colorado, Missouri

oak roots spread beneath sidewalks, force
concrete slabs up at strange angles
create cracks, ridges & hazards

46

squirrels snicker, chuckle & squawk

scamper up tree trunks across limbs

& boughs, jump from trees to fence-tops

sprint across lawns, duck under hedges

& shrubs, scurry along sidewalks

with acorns gripped between teeth, zig-

zag across the boulevard, dance

along black powerlines with erect

tails, descend onto leaf-strewn lawns

burrow into brown grass with front paws

digging up worms, swivel heads & prick

ears when dogs bark & cars brake, chase

each other up the alley, squat

atop blue recycling bins, grip

branches swaying in the wind, bouncing

beneath their weight, leap from rooftops

speed like furry arrows through the air

47

dust, leaves & pollen coat
a bronze Toyota Land Cruiser

with a red & white VIVA
TERLINGUA bumper sticker

parked in front of a collapsing
white wooden garage beneath

green & blonde bamboo encroaching
from the neighboring property

leaning over the eight-foot-tall
rickety cedar paling fence

like the neighborhood gossip
arching over the cracked concrete driveway

an organic arbor shading entropy

48

a ninety-year-old ranch-style
three-bedroom family home

with a front porch swing
white siding & black shutters

surrounded by mature trees
manicured green lawns, weedless

flowerbeds bursting with violets
on a large corner lot sells

at auction to developers
after the owner's death

demolished, bulldozed, erased
the prime lot cleared & scraped

prepared to maximize profit
family & neighborhood

history destroyed to make
way for a three-story ten-

bedroom ten-bathroom student
apartment building boasting

contemporary styling
sleek modern appliances

high-speed internet, parking
for eight vehicles, balconies

security cameras, a roof-
top party deck, grill & fire

pit, easy access to shops
bars, restaurants & campus

the future of urban living

49

a twentysomething woman cruises
the boulevard on her skateboard

brown hair braided, eyes hidden
behind sunglasses, ears plugged

with earbuds, bare brown arms
loose & relaxed, knees slightly

bent, blue jeans ripped, red
Converse facing south as she rides

west, black backpack hanging
from bare shoulders, white

tank top rippling in the breeze
mouth formed into a half-smile

hips & board swaying & weaving
as youth seizes the autumn day

50

leaves turn burgundy, yellow & brown
in bright Sunday afternoon autumn sun

workers blow leaves into the boulevard
let the wind take them into other yards

cats bathe in sunshine on front lawns beneath
clear blue skies, residents stroll hand in hand

along the neighborhood's sidewalks, revel
in seventy-degree temperatures

red, blue, black, gray & white parked cars reflect
afternoon light, fallen leaves cover lawns

sidewalks & driveways, blanket calm backyards
peaked roofs & eaves cast shadows across lawns

neighborhood cats stalk insects in alleys
fallen leaves trail behind passing vehicles

51

on gamedays, frat boys & sorority

girls gather on the corner

of University & the boulevard

clutch red solo cups as they stand

drinking in clusters, the boys wearing

purple polo shirts & khakis

the girls wearing cowgirl boots, short skirts

& purple dresses, get drunk

in the morning sun, stumble

to the stadium before kickoff

52

the homeowner on the corner

of the boulevard & Park Ridge

installs BIDEN 2020 signs

at each corner of his triangular

lot, carefully inserts two small

American flags into the top

of each sign, declares his allegiance

53

a navy-blue Audi Q5

with a sorority sticker

on the rear window

pulls into a driveway

a young blonde woman

wearing a baggy t-shirt

obscuring whatever might

be underneath hops out

of the SUV holding

a smartphone & a purse

opens the rear driver's-

side door, releases a golden

retriever puppy, follows

as it bounds across the lawn

pauses to squat, shit on dry

fallen orange autumn leaves

54

smoke billows from a rental house
backyard at 8:22 am

on gameday, brisket smoking
& scenting the neighborhood

young male football fans adorned
in purple & white jerseys

arrive in SUVS at 9am
exit vehicles clutching six-packs
of light beer & breakfast tacos

the street fills with cars, trucks
& SUVS parked nose to tail
beside curbs, crammed two-deep

into short driveways, rear ends
hanging out in the street

55

seventeen young women wearing

cut-off jean shorts, tight khaki

skirts, purple & white crop

tops & cowgirl boots stagger

along the boulevard

through late afternoon light

grasp red plastic cups

iPhones & each other's arms

weave from the concrete curb

across the asphalt to the faded

white painted center line

laugh, gesticulate & gossip

56

police arrive in four black
& white SUVs, break
up a student gameday party

on the corner of Stadium
& the boulevard
students emerge in packs

from the front door
& backyard, disperse
throughout the neighborhood

check phones in search
of the next event, migrate
in flocks towards parties

in progress four blocks east

57

college girls sipping green

twenty-four-ounce cans

of Founder's IPA

saunter beside the curb

the voice of the announcer

carries on the wind

horns & sirens blast

signaling a hometeam touchdown

58

three days after the election

a brand-new American flag

appears on a pole beside

a retired homeowner's

front door, clean, bright, crisp

a blue surgical mask lies

crumpled in the gutter

the wind blows a white

plastic Kroger bag down

the middle of the boulevard

vehicles pass with masks

dangling from rearview mirrors

a FOR SALE sign appears

in front of the empty house

on the corner of Greene

piles of autumn leaves form

behind parked cars

sheltering from the wind

59

a thirtysomething

man with curly black

hair cruises the boulevard

on a vintage bike

brown leather satchel

slung over the right shoulder

of his rumpled black

velvet jacket, leans

back over his rear wheel, zig-

zags to the corner

of Cockrell, turns right

rides north towards the library

60

three brown men in a canary-
yellow twenty-four-foot Ford F-
350 moving truck arrive
at the white-brick house

with the terracotta roof
on the corner of Greene, park
on the north side of the boulevard

facing west, take eight-foot
aluminum ladders & ten-
foot lengths of gutter from the truck

set the ladders up against the side
of the house between trimmed green
hedges & flowerless crepe myrtles

climb towards terracotta tiles
with brown leather tool belts swinging
tear down rusty old gutters

with gloved hands, dismantle downpipes
with ease, shout instructions in Spanish
install new gutters with screaming

power drills, grind metal screws
through aluminum gutters
into wooden eaves, bathe

in the reflection of autumn
afternoon sunshine off painted
white bricks, shield eyes with sunglasses

& trucker caps, measure
tighten, craft work to endure
seasons & years, apply
energy & skill to material

61

autumn leaves fall from the oak
revealing a nest high above

the lawn, newly visible
against a crisp blue sky, standing

out at boughs' end like a white
stitch on a black seam, shaping

a new afternoon shadow
remaining within sight

until spring brings a new veil
of curtaining emerald leaves

62

the local high school marching
band beats and blares across

the boulevard on homecoming
morning, wakes homeowners

draws curious residents
to windows & front porches

sends beats & horn-blasts
echoing from brick walls

soundwaves ricocheting
around the boulevard

broadcasts energy
& excitement around

the locked-down neighborhood

63

the poet & professor's

son picks up lopped limbs

twigs & leaves from the lawn

stacks the largest beside the curb

drops smaller pieces into brown

leaf bags, performs his chores

like a professional landscaper

preparing the property

for Thanksgiving guests

64

a silver Dodge Ram pick-up

travelling west on the boulevard

slows, pulls over to the curb

followed by a black Nissan Sentra

easing in behind. the drivers

exit their vehicles, stride towards

each other, stop, embrace & kiss

exchange saliva for dozens

of seconds, separate, step back

three feet, argue, gesticulate

shake heads, look away from each other

lean forearms on the truck for a long

moment, turn & walk away

climb back into driver's seats

65

two weeks into the pandemic

George ties a white ribbon around

the live oak in front of his house

declares his support for his daughter

& her colleagues treating covid

patients in the hospitals. eight

long months into the pandemic

covid kills George's sister one

day after Thanksgiving, ends her

seventy-two-year life as temps

drop & frigid winds blow. dying

leaves from the white-ribboned live oak

cover George's lawn with a pall

66

electricity

internet & cable

lines connect poles & posts

to houses, garages

& garden sheds, cross

fences & rooftops

bisect trees from Trinity

Episcopalian church

at the western end

to the used car dealership

beside the railway line

at the eastern end

all along the boulevard

the cables & wires hum

& buzz *only connect!*

67

the tall blonde college student

reverses her white Mercedes

E-350 into the driveway

positions her luxury

car nose forward, displays curves

tinted windows & sunroof

glittering rims, aggressive

angles for public perusal

positions precision German

engineering & styling

for an effortless exit

68

grey metal guardrails surround

a locked signal box on a concrete

traffic island at the eastern

terminus of the boulevard

yellow-painted curbs, sidewalkless

sections, narrow overgrown alleys

lead north between back fences

cars park in oak-shade beside concrete

curbs, dead oak leaves accumulate

in gutters, residents stash trash

bins in alleys behind garage

apartments like family secrets

69

a silver-gold Volkswagen

Jetta pulls over to the curb

on the southside of the boulevard

the driver looks at his smartphone

for twenty seconds before driving

away to his secret rendezvous

70

wooden floors inside houses

vibrate as freight trains cross

the eastern terminus

of the boulevard. the blast

of the train horns carries

seven blocks west, the rumble

of wheels transporting boxcars

& shipping containers south

to the gulf audible inside

houses a quarter mile away

71

runners weave through shadows

under the avenue

of trees along cracked side-

walks, stride from slab

to slab, avoid

tree roots & puddles

leap like mountain

goats over hazards

settle into relaxed

cadences on smooth

stretches, transport

selves into the zone

72

a blonde toddler runs north

across dry brown winter grass

in Worth Hills Park towards

the boulevard chasing

a bouncing red plastic

ball the size of his head

the boy's mother chases

him towards traffic, arms

stretched forwards, yells *stop!*

as a charcoal Audi Q5

drives towards the toddler

from the west coming home

from the school run, slows

to almost-walking-pace

as the distance between

the toddler & the vehicle

decreases & tiny arms

embrace the captured ball

lift it joyfully skywards

as the mother's hands land

on the toddler's shoulders

& she makes eye contact

with the Audi driver

eyes and mouth wide

73

buzzards wheel through cold blue

December sky, bank & glide on arctic

currents, circle leafless grey oaks searching

for new roadkill on the boulevard below

swoop down to the grass verge

where Bermuda knits through Buffalo

rip into the brown squirrel carcass

74

snow falls on the boulevard
coats Mercedes, Porsches & Audis

rests upon dormant lawns, melts
on grey concrete sidewalks & driveways

accumulates on red tiled roofs
reclines on hedges, black iron

railings, mailboxes, falls
diagonally through leafless

oaks, overlays jacuzzi covers
outdoor furniture, blue pool

covers, deluxe stainless-steel grills
backyard brick-paved paths, half-pipes

woodpiles, vegetable gardens
recycling bins, trampolines

garages, carports, swing sets
flowerbeds, piles of dead brown

leaves, whitens the neighborhood
for the first time in seven years

75

an ambulance parks in front

of a house on the corner

of University

& the boulevard, lights

flashing. EMTs wheel

a stretcher to the front door

76

the boulevard is quiet today. cars

are stationary. silence descends. dead

leaves bathe in stillness, recline in gutters.

doors remain closed. blinds stay drawn. bare boughs

& trunks rest against grey skies, appear black

& sullen. powerlines refuse to sway

& dance. security lights disperse soft

light. the red bow on the black mailbox fails

to flutter. squirrels, birds & cats seek

silent shelter from the glacial morning

like exiles trapped in the wrong hemisphere

ACKNOWLEDGEMENTS

Section 46 appeared as "Furry Arrows" in *The Quarantine Review*, issue 8 (May 2021), p. 45.

Sections 53 and 59 appeared as "Golden" and "Scholarship" in *Melbourne Culture Corner*, volume 1, issue 6 (February 2021), p. 3.

Section 61 appeared as "Emerald" in *Bealtaine Magazine*, issue 1 (Spring 2021), p. 6.

Section 73 appeared as "Winter Feast" in *Drunk Monkeys* (2021).

Thanks always to my partner Tricia and our daughter Celeste, and to my parents Paul and Moira O'Reilly. Huge thanks to Sean Scarisbrick for his insightful comments on an earlier version of the manuscript, and for three decades of mateship! It's a privilege to have such a perceptive and honest first reader.

I wish to thank the following people for friendship, support, opportunities and inspiration: Lachlan Brown, Shane Strange, rob mclennan, Alex Lemon, Damien Donnelly, Annemarie Ní Churreáin, Jessica Traynor, Matt Hohner, Anne Casey, Mark Roberts, Cedrick May, Penny Ingram, David Bonnet, Aisling Keogh, Mari Maxwell, Cassandra Atherton and Kevin Bateman.

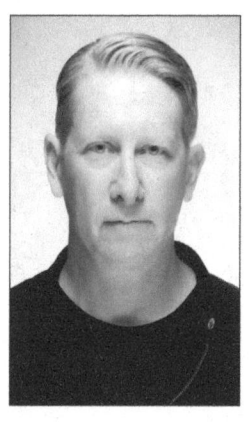

ABOUT THE AUTHOR
NATHANAEL O'REILLY

Irish-Australian poet Nathanael O'Reilly teaches creative writing at the University of Texas at Arlington. His poetry collections include *Selected Poems of Ned Kelly* (Downingfield Press, 2024), *Landmarks* (Lamar University Literary Press, 2024), *Dear Nostalgia* (above/ground press, 2023), *(Un)belonging* (Recent Work Press, 2020), *BLUE* (above/ground press, 2020) and *Preparations for Departure* (University of Western Australia Publishing, 2017). His work appears in 125 journals and anthologies published in 15 countries, including *Cordite Poetry Review*, *The Honest Ulsterman*, *Mascara Literary Review*, *New World Writing Quarterly*, *Southword: New International Writing*, *Trasna*, *Westerly* and *Wisconsin Review*. He is poetry editor for *Antipodes: A Global Journal of Australian/New Zealand Literature*.